LORRIES IN BRITAIN
THE 1990s

CARL JOHNSON

AMBERLEY

First published 2023

Amberley Publishing
The Hill, Stroud
Gloucestershire, GL5 4EP

www.amberley-books.com

Copyright © Carl Johnson, 2023

The right of Carl Johnson to be identified as the Author of this work has been asserted in accordance with the Copyrights, Designs and Patents Act 1988.

ISBN 978 1 3981 0082 4 (print)
ISBN 978 1 3981 0083 1 (ebook)

All rights reserved. No part of this book may be reprinted or reproduced or utilised in any form or by any electronic, mechanical or other means, now known or hereafter invented, including photocopying and recording, or in any information storage or retrieval system, without the permission in writing from the Publishers.

British Library Cataloguing in Publication Data.
A catalogue record for this book is available from the British Library.

Origination by Amberley Publishing.
Printed in the UK.

Introduction

Following on from an earlier volume of vehicles in the 1980s, this book contains another selection of photographs, all captured by the author, of lorries seen in the UK during the 1990s.

These really were times of change. Many of the UK manufacturers were struggling to keep pace with these changes, and were also trying hard to compete with the influx of imported vehicles, especially from Europe.

Indeed, the decade was to see the end of Leyland, who had in fact been involved with DAF of Eindhoven since 1987. The receivers were called in at the beginning of February 1993. A management buyout saved them in June of that year, but by 1998 they had been taken over by Paccar, who already owned the Sandbach manufacturer Foden. By the next decade neither the Leyland or Foden names were in use, and they remain missed by users and enthusiasts alike.

ERF, another Sandbach manufacturer, was sold initially to Western Star in 1996. Although major investment was put into a new factory in nearby Middlewich, they were also struggling and were sold on to MAN in 2000. Dennis (established 1895) are well known for producing lorries, buses and municipal vehicles but have long since dropped their goods range. Indeed, to this day Dennis are still in business and focus on municipals, although they too are now part of a larger group – Terberg Environmental B.V., whose head office is in the Netherlands.

However, still to be seen dutifully earning their keep in the 1990s was a lot of what enthusiasts consider to be classics of the time.

A lot of UK haulage companies had by this time already tested the water with foreign 'seed' vehicles. These were often offered at discounted rates and were put head-to-head with established makes to facilitate comparisons on factors such as operating costs and fuel consumption. The industry was changing in many ways, and at the start of the decade there were approximately 480,000 lorries registered for use on UK roads. By 2022 that number had been reduced to approximately 415,000, a reduction of around 14 per cent. This is in part due to the increase in the maximum gross vehicle weight (GVW) of articulated vehicles to 44 tonnes.

The 1990s also saw legislation being changed with the DVLA introducing the theory test (1996) as part of the process to obtain a full driving licence. Then, potential lorry drivers had to progress to the heavy goods vehicle tests, which were set at different classes for rigid and articulated vehicles. In 1992, due to an EU directive, the terminology for lorries changed from HGV (heavy goods vehicle) to

LGV (large goods vehicle). The UK had previously designated LGV (light goods vehicle) for vehicles under 7.5 tonnes gross. Another EU directive introduced speed limiters for all new goods vehicles registered from 1 August 1992, the limiters being calibrated to 56 mph.

There was, and still is, some controversy over the introduction of limiters, where the obvious safety aspect has to be considered. A lot of drivers find that bunching up of lorries on the roads occurs, and, two lorries side by side on a dual carriageway often causes frustration for other road users.

Another major event in the 1990s was the opening of the Channel Tunnel between the UK and France. A major project, it had long been suggested that a tunnel be constructed – the very first was apparently an idea from Napoleon Bonaparte. After several false starts the current tunnel opened in 1994 and has reduced the travelling time significantly. The cross-Channel ferries are still operational, and some drivers prefer this option as they can have a longer rest period. One downside to this increase in inter-continental movements is foreign vehicles coming over to the UK.

These have lower overheads than the UK operators and while in the UK they often take on work by offering cheaper rates. This unfair advantage is called 'cabotage'.

Another thing worth a mention though is the worldwide increase of the ISO shipping containers. This way of moving goods has certainly seen major changes; the old ports and docks as we knew them have changed forever with the labour force of dockers and stevedores being greatly reduced. The infrastructure of a lot of ports has seen major investments to cope with the handling and storage of the containers, with several hauliers investing in outfits with twist-lock skeletal trailers to transport them.

So, let's take a browse through a period of time, and, take a look at the vehicles that could be found during this decade. Fortunately, there is a very active preservation scene with clubs and societies being formed, so lots of the vehicle makes and types featured in this volume can be seen at the numerous events and road runs that are held throughout the UK.

Lorries in Britain: The 1990s　　5

What better way to start than to see these two ERF 64G (LV cab) lorries of R. & R. Limbert of Altrincham, Cheshire. GMB 537G, chassis 16653, was new to Wilds Motors in 1968. UMB 404J, chassis 20270, was new to Ralston Transport in 1970. Both lorries were over twenty years old and still working when the photo was taken in 1992.

Of course, all lorries can be subject to mechanical failure and unfortunately sometimes even worse, an accident. This Scammell Crusader of Whitakers from Spalding was on standby for such events when the yard was visited in May 1993.

Keeping company with the Scammell at Whitakers was this somewhat rare ex-military Leyland Martian six-wheel recovery vehicle. These 6 x 6 all-wheel drive vehicles were handy on recovery work. However, they were quite thirsty with the original straight eight-cylinder petrol engines!

1992 and this Leyland Marathon, fitted with a day cab, was spotted on Clay Cross Industrial estate. It was owned by a company from Saffron Walden, Essex who used the artic display unit to promote their business. Presumably it had been parked 'up country' between shows?

It's always nice to get a photograph of a lorry going about its business. This working shot of chassis number 47587 is an ERF C25 double drive six-wheel tipper of M.J. Napper & Sons, Bristol. It was discharging its load of hardcore at Denslow's yard in Chard, Somerset in July 1993.

In 1986, Iveco had purchased a majority (52 per cent) of shares in the commercial division of the Ford Motor Company. The Ford Cargo was never a major player as a maximum weight artic, but this particular example of A.V. Dawson Ltd of Middlesbrough was giving good service when seen in 1993. The dual branding was an obvious exercise.

Graham Durber had for a number of years been in the business of people moving. First with Durber's Taxis, and later with several coaches when he used only his first name. Graham's Coaches had this fine Foden S39 eight-wheel recovery vehicle that was used both as the company standby, and also for any recovery work that cropped up in the area.

Dale Farm is part of a farmer's co-operative that is owned by over 1,300 dairy farmers. The Leyland Constructor was always a popular choice as a rigid eight-wheel tipper, but to see one in van form was a little unusual. This example was caught on camera at the Ferrybridge services, which is a popular comfort stop close to the M62 and the A1.

The 'invasion' of foreign vehicles was mentioned in the introduction and this Scania 93M is such an example. The author was on a night out at Truck Haven, Carnforth when this drawbar outfit of Thacker Barrows turned up. The driver was no doubt looking forward to a night in the sleeper pod over the cab!

A sign of the times way back in the 1990s was the rope and sheet method to cover the loads. This, of course, was to change with the curtainside bodies becoming more popular. The old established firm of Jack Richards was running this ERF C Series in 1992. By 1997 it had been sold to Allmans Transport of Congleton.

Bostock's of Congleton were staunch users of classic lorries, including this comparatively rare Atkinson Raider. At a mere sixteen years young when the photograph was taken, the vehicle looked extremely tidy. Fitted with a Gardner 6LXB 180 bhp engine, it shows how reliable and long serving these vehicles were.

Another of Bostock's fine vehicles, this time an Atkinson Searcher six-wheel curtainside lorry, again with the Gardner 180 engine. These engines were good on fuel, so with the twin fuel tanks this lorry would have a good range of miles without having to top up. The lorry was new to Wilds Motors of Altrincham.

Lorries in Britain: The 1990s 11

Beresford Transport of Tunstall, Stoke on Trent were a long-established haulier and one of the first to do Continental work. The company closed in the 1990s with the Continental operation going to Bassett's of Tittensor. This DAF 2100 six-wheeler was used on the 'Supersheds' contract and was something of a rarity in the fleet.

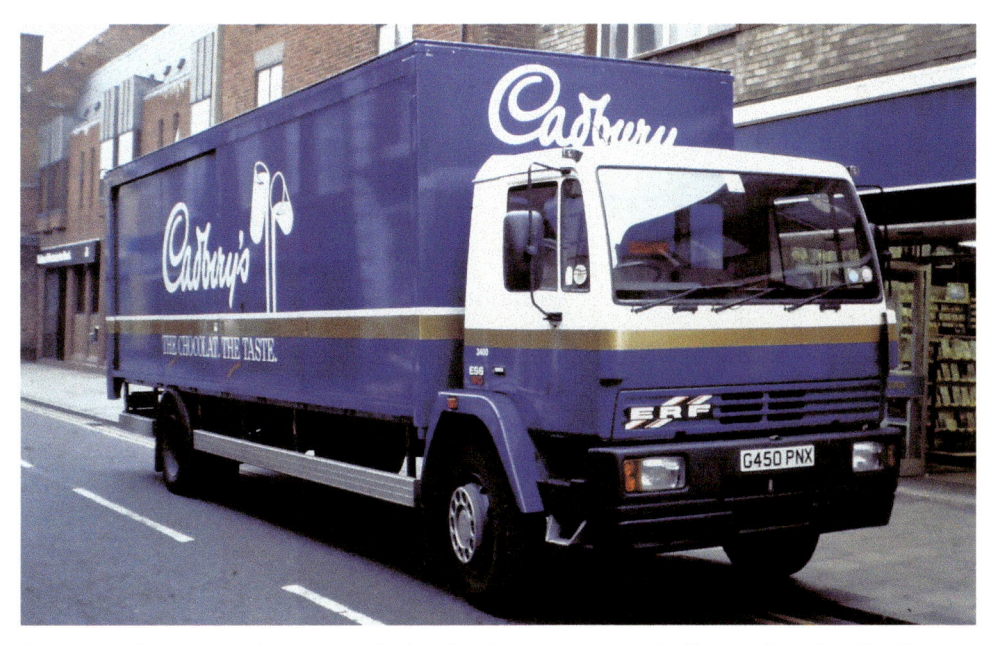

An extremely attractive livery is applied to this fine ERF ES6 on Cadbury's chocolate distribution. The ES range had the all-steel cab manufactured by Steyr of Austria and was offered as an alternative to ERF's steel/plastic (SP) cab. The vehicle was photographed on 10 October 1991 on Cheadle (Staffs) high street.

A division of Redland was for the manufacture of bricks. This Foden 4300 eight-wheeler (with crane) from that operation was taking a break on the A1 near Retford, Nottinghamshire. The curtain sides were another system introduced for load restraint, cargo nets being the preceding method.

Another Foden 4300 of Redland, this time from the roof tile division. The lorry was seen at Grampound Road, Cornwall and is coupled to a 'pup' trailer, the crane being mounted on the rear of the lorry to enable offloading of both the lorry and the trailer. The load restraints differ a little from the previous lorry.

Lorries in Britain: The 1990s 13

And yet another Foden 4300 from the Redland organisation, this time an eight-wheel tipper from the aggregates division. This was taking a weekend break on the Barton lorry park, Richmond, Yorkshire one Sunday in May 1993.

The world's largest Yorkie bars? These two ERF E14 artics were taking a mandatory break one Saturday morning at The Farm Café on the A17 in Lincolnshire on 27 June 1992. Apparently, it was regular stop for the Nestle's distribution drivers from the York Rowntree's factory.

The author's vehicle when doing a bit of casual driving, the manhole rings were from Leek in Staffordshire and the photo was taken on arrival at a building site in Leeds. Observers may think there is little in the form of load restraints, but the rings were scotched to the platform as well as the ropes with the traditional 'hitch' knots.

Moss & Lovatt had been loyal to the Leyland marque for a number of years before changing over to ERF, a make used until the firm closed. This Leyland Marathon 2, a day cab artic, is another loaded with Hughes Concrete products from Leek. Hughes too have also closed. Keeping it company in the yard were two Leyland Clydesdales that had been retired.

Lorries in Britain: The 1990s   15

This Leyland Marathon, although looking a little beat up and not taxed, was still in use as a yard shunter at G.W. Sissons & Son Ltd of Sherburn in Elmet, North Yorkshire. Lots of haulage companies used to pension off their old vehicles for such duties. The unit was ten years old when photographed in the yard in 1992.

The Scammell Crusader was a popular vehicle with some operators including BRS and the British Army. With the Mk 3 Motor Panels cab they were quite a handsome design. Available with several engine options, this one was seeing out its days with Sissons in the yard. The trade plates in the window suggest it may have been used to shunt trailers and maybe to take them for the annual testing.

A nice mix and match outfit is seen here. The ERF EC11 just about scrapes into the decade. Of interest is the tractor unit which is in the old livery of W.R. Wood Haulage of Ashbourne, Derby. The company was taken over by Turners of Soham and the vehicle was still based in Ashbourne to service the cement works of Blue Circle. Even the Blue Circle livery has long since gone.

One Sunday in 1992 a visit to Brandon Creek in Norfolk was undertaken, and spotted at the Bibby's' feed mill was this Foden 4300 eight-wheel bulk tipper looking rather clean and smart – and no doubt chomping at the bit ready to face the next day's work.

Just outside Crewe's town centre and in a regular parking place for lorries was this Leyland DAF 95-310 of Quantock Transport Ltd. It is coupled to a bulk powder tank trailer. The company specialised in this work and previously had traded as Brown Bros of North Rode.

Part of Staveley Industries was Salter, who did weighbridge testing. This Scammell Routeman Mk 3 would have had a pretty tough life as it would be fully loaded with test weights throughout its life. It is seen here at the British Salt premises at Middlewich, who were also part of the Staveley Group. The vehicle was by then seventeen years old.

In comparison to the previous photograph, we see how weighbridge testing had changed its methods. The Scammell of Salter had a travelling hoist on a beam inside the body to lift the weights; here we see a Hiab crane, which would make the job a lot quicker. The Foden 4350 of Staffordshire County Council was working in Sandbach at the time.

A. Rose & Son Ltd of Newark were well known for running elderly classic vehicles. This Scammell Handyman Mk 3 unit was still in use when twelve years old. The fibreglass Michelotti-designed cab on these vehicles were quite a revelation when introduced way back in the 1960s.

Lorries in Britain: The 1990s   19

Another of Rose's fine-looking machines. This too is a Scammell. However this model, initially known as the Routeman 4, was to morph into the Leyland Constructor as the Scammell name was removed. Manufactured at Watford it was marketed by Leyland and was a popular choice as a tipper. The goods chassis, as seen here, was less popular.

John Dickinson, based at the old Winston station near Darlington, County Durham, did a lot of work carrying construction machines, mainly for Caterpillar. These two ERF E14 artics were set up loaded for delivery when seen in the yard in 1993. Of note are the differences and modifications on the SP cab.

When photographed this ERF 68GXB was still in daily service at twenty years old. An owner-driver, Don Hobson ran it often coupled to a drawbar trailer. The 'heck' over the cab would have been used when carrying straw. Fortunately, this lorry went into preservation and can still be seen at shows.

Lisa the Dodge K Series was looking a little work worn when seen back in the operator's yard in 1991. However, the vehicle was still in use, at over twenty years old, for household coal deliveries. As well as this vehicle, the owners also operated bulk tippers and were active in the realms of preservation.

Arthur Wright and Son of Weston Coyney, Stoke on Trent were originally scrap metal dealers. A move was made into waste products and this Leyland Bison with a 'rolonof' type skip was just about to set off to change over the skip at a nearby customers.

Markham Moor services on the A1 is where this ex-Foden demonstrator was seen. It is a Foden 4350 and although it retained the 'demo' livery it had passed to the M.S. Wayman fleet, based at Sutton Bridge in Lincolnshire. All their vehicles were named after the nearby river. This one, *Nene Crusader*, was piloted by *Peter*.

Ed Weetman from Great Haywood, Staffs has a large fleet of bulk tippers. This Scania 82M rigid eight-wheeler is in the original fleet livery. Later on, it was repainted into the Criddle Billington colours – a company that Weetman's did a lot of work for delivering animal feeds to local farms.

A typical outfit of Weetman's is this artic bulk tipper. Employed mostly on animal feed the DAF 3300 was in a minority on the fleet as at that time they had ERF, Volvo and Scania as preferred makes. The premises also have large warehousing and a public weighbridge.

Referred to in the USA as a 'cabover' this left-hand drive White Road Boss 2 of R.D. Johnson was a little unusual to find on Ferrybridge Services. Not many American vehicles were to be seen working in the UK, and this one was engaged on container movements for Bell shipping. The name *Top Cat* suggests a Caterpillar engine provided the horsepower?

Another container haulier, this Foden 4300 was operated by Mark & Rory, the Cooke Bros. The photograph was taken at the old Poplar Café at Lymm in Cheshire in 1993. Just twelve months later the new Poplar with more modern facilities was opened nearby.

Badged as a Bison 2, which was a six-wheel model, we have here a Leyland skip lorry seen having a break at the Farm Café on the A17. So, maybe it had been cut down to two axles, or has it been re-cabbed. Or maybe even just a bit of 'badge engineering'?

What is believed to be an ex-Ashton Vernon vehicle, this Leyland Constructor 30-25 was often parked at weekends at this location in Congleton, Cheshire. The name on the cab door has been covered over but I.H. Jordan appears on the headboard. 'Julie Ann', scribed on the bumper, was no doubt an acquaintance of the driver.

Lorries in Britain: The 1990s   25

Still with trade plates in the cab and waiting its first duty is this ERF ES8 six-wheel tipper of Frank Tucker from Heavitree, Exeter. Tuckers were in fact an ERF dealer and obviously at the time large users of the marque. Other vehicles on the fleet were in customer liveries like Tarmac-Westbrick and English China Clays (ECC).

A very pleasing line up for any lorry enthusiast! H. Crabtree Ltd from New Mills near Stockport had two yards in the area. This one was a little cramped but was home to these three Sandbach products, two Foden's and an ERF, all tucked neatly away for the weekend. They had a number of these makes and also some Leylands on the fleet.

G.C.S. Johnson from Barton, Richmond, North Yorkshire does a lot of heavy haulage work. This DAF 2800 ATI 6 x 2 artic low-loader, with sleeper cab was seen back in 1993 on the Barton industrial estate loaded with a Komatsu 360-degree excavator.

Walston Poultry Farm Ltd has a number of interests in the Blandford, Dorset area breeding chickens and supplying eggs. The Friend family were owners and directors. This day cab Bedford TM with a single axle trailer was used to carry live chickens. The TM had been in production since 1973 until 1986, when Bedford was sold to AWD.

At the other end of the poultry chain was the supply of products for human consumption. One company engaged on this work was Grampian. We see here one of their Seddon Atkinson Strato artic fridge vans, which was transhipping some of the load into another of the company's vehicles on the Poplar Café at Lymm, Cheshire.

Fleet number M4485 of Pickfords was this ERF E6 removals van that was very often to be seen at the Stoke on Trent depot. The European operation was part of the Allied International network, and although the Pickfords name is prominent the Allied logo can be seen towards the rear of the vehicle.

Number 751 on the hymn sheet at Linkman, Runcorn was this narrow cab Foden 3325 artic fuel tanker. Linkman was part of the Transport Development Group (TDG) and is seen wearing the 'Juggler' livery and logos. In 2011 with approval from the European Commission the company was sold to Norbert Dentressangle.

Old school haulage, this Atkinson Borderer artic was twenty years old when seen in Tudor's yard at Branston, Burton on Trent. The well-worked look, the sleeper pod, and the flat trailer is typical of how it used to be. An absolute delight to the die-hard enthusiast!

Lorries in Britain: The 1990s 29

The Volvo F86 was introduced in the mid-1960s and had a long production run. This one was registered in 1971 and had been adapted to carry racecars. Ken Ferriday is based in Ashbourne where the vehicle was captured on film on the old (now defunct) lorry park.

A nice looking Foden 4300 6 x 2 unit of Orbell Kings Lynn (OKL). It is coupled to a refrigerated van trailer that sports a popular name of a pasta sauce producer that most readers should recognise. Dolmio is actually a registered trademark of Mars Incorporated. The brand was introduced by Masterfoods in 1985 in Australia before being launched in Scotland.

The transport division of English China Clays, St Austell, Cornwall (now Imerys) was known as Heavy Transport (ECC) Ltd. This ERF C31 eight-wheel tipper was based at Scarne, Launceston. It is seen here undergoing maintenance at Pannell Commercials, who were actually Seddon Atkinson dealers.

1993, and while at Pannell Commercials in Launceston, there was an opportunity to capture their recovery vehicles on film. The first seen was this Scammell Crusader six-wheeler. The company was one of the main recovery vehicle operators in the area, with the busy A30 being a mere stone's throw away.

The other recovery vehicle seen at the time was this fantastic looking Atkinson 'Silver Knight' BT7566C, which is also a six-wheeler. Quite a rare machine in this bonneted layout, the Mk 2 cab is fitted. Originally it was designed as a heavy-duty tractor plated for 75 tons GCW, and it is fitted with a Cummins 250 bhp engine.

Brit European was founded in 1924 as W. Carman & Son. Pioneers in cross-Channel movements, they are a major player to this day with offices on the Continent as well as the UK. This MAN close-coupled drawbar outfit was one of several ordered with an underfloor engine to keep the overall height down to accommodate high volume bodies. This one was based in Zeebrugge but was caught on camera in the UK.

Showing a little rust around the cab, this six-wheel K Series Dodge recovery vehicle was on station at Charnwood M1 Truck Centre at Shepshed, Leicestershire. As suggested in the name, the M1 motorway was just minutes away from the base.

On a north-east safari, this Foden Haulmaster eight-wheel flat platform lorry with the S10 Mk 1 cab was spotted in Wolsingham, County Durham. John Suddes was a relatively small operator with just an ERF artic keeping the Foden company at that time.

Lorries in Britain: The 1990s 33

The author's friend John Andrew, of Tregadillet in Cornwall, provided the drivers for these Leyland Roadtrains of Tesco. Later on, the operation expanded and served the Cornish supermarkets. These two were actually shunted down at the time from Westbury in Wiltshire to Tregadillet before final delivery.

Turner Waldrum Transport of Shepshed, Leicestershire had this Foden 6 x 2 4350 artic calling in for fuel at the Junction 23 Truckstop at Shepshed in March 1992. At the time a number of lorries seemed to be based there – maybe this was one of them?

Cheadle High Street, Staffordshire is the scene for this recovery operation for the local bus company known then as Potteries Motor Traction (PMT). A scene not possible today as the high street is now one way in the opposite direction. The Leyland Bison was equipped with the popular Holmes twin boom recovery gear.

Of course, all vehicles need an occasional wash – but not all operators have their own facility. This ERF C Series artic of Browns of Stoke in the Building Adhesives livery (BAL) was going through the company's wash after coming in from its week's work.

In Durham's yard at Billingham near Stockton on Tees, County Durham was this Atkinson Borderer in Sanderson livery. In use as a yard shunter, it was in good condition; so much so that the vehicle did in fact go into preservation.

Helsby & Longden are a well-established transport and distribution company. Founded in 1926, the company was based in Frodsham where this Seddon Atkinson 3-11 artic was photographed. The tri-axle flat trailer with sheeted load is almost a thing of the past now.

Quite rare in the UK was the Pegaso Troner. This example of Harrison's from Tarleton was seen on Sandbach Services. The Troner had been introduced in 1987 and was the last model built by Pegaso. In fact the the photograph was taken during the last year of production, 1993.

The longevity of ERF lorries is well documented; these three had only recently been pensioned off by Parks Potatoes of Macclesfield in 1993. The combined age of these at the time being no less than sixty-nine years! Luckily all of them have survived.

Lorries in Britain: The 1990s   37

With the S10 Mk 5 cab this Foden 4300 eight-wheel tipper certainly looked the part. On contract to Wimpey Hobbs the vehicle was owned by R. & D. Curley of Bristol and was seen in the quarry at Halecombe, Frome, Somerset when on a south-west safari.

Pidduck & Beardmore from Longport, Stoke on Trent had a number of interests including steel stockists, builders' merchants and ironmongery. This locally registered double-drive Foden 4350 was coupled up to a trailer for the carriage of bricks and blocks. The company closed in 2003.

With a twisted front bumper, it looks like the rigours of building sites have taken its toll on this DAF 2500 of D.B. Haulage. The vehicle had just been loaded one Saturday morning and was returning to the yard of Shepperson's at Somercotes, Alfreton, Derby's.

Of the same format as the previous lorry, we see another DAF 2500 eight-wheel flat platform lorry. Both have a centre-mounted crane for off-loading. This one was from the J. Shepperson fleet. Both photographs were taken in 1992.

Somewhat rare were these Seddon Atkinson Strato artic tippers that were in the Tunstall, Stoke on Trent dealership (Mainline Trucks) for servicing. They are multi-drive outfits that have driven trailer axles as well as the tractor unit, making them very handy on unmade ground.

James Leech & Co. from Haslington, Crewe do a lot of delivery work for Mornflake Oats in nearby Crewe. On a visit to their yard, we were diverted and escorted over to the mill in Gresty Road, where we took a few photos. One vehicle seen was this Leyland Freighter 15-16 curtainsider. Since then, the livery of Mornflake has changed to orange.

Tucked away in a side street in Burton on Trent the author spotted this Atkinson Borderer recovery vehicle of D.A. Elliot & Sons. Trading as Elliot Vehicle Services Ltd, the company were engaged in vehicle modifications and repairs. No doubt this motor came in handy at times!

1991, and no fewer than six Ergomatic cab Leyland Buffalo tractor units were to be found still in service at Browns of Tunstall. The original Buffalos had the ill-fated fixed-head 500 engines, but these Mk 2 versions would either have the L11 or the TL11 fitted.

Lorries in Britain: The 1990s 41

No book would be complete without a reference to the famous Eddie Stobart. This Ford/IVECO Cargo close-coupled drawbar outfit was seen at a small depot in Wisbech, Cambs. *Eileen* is in the old, and some say much favoured, style of livery.

And let's have another Stobart outfit. Fleet number H759, a Mercedes Benz Actros 1835, was on Hartshead Moor Services. It is in the livery of a major customer at the time, United Glass. For many years United were serviced by the famous Robson's of Carlisle.

Originally from the much-missed fleet of Sam Longson from Chapel-en-le-Frith, this Atkinson Defender eight-wheel tipper passed to Stan Frodsham of Upper Hulme and was worked by him as an owner-driver until retirement. It fell into disrepair and was offered as a lot in an auction back in January 2021. Its current whereabouts are not known.

Birch Services on the M62, and an enforced tachograph break when the author was driving saw this fine Atkinson artic doing likewise. The unit is a standard Atkinson Borderer with an added axle and the Cummins 250 engine (rated at 228 bhp). Rumour has it that the vehicle still exists.

Another make that was comparatively rare in the UK was the Austrian-built Steyr lorries. This artic fridge van of Angus Cochrane from Northern Ireland was on the Ferrybridge Services. The company sold out to Montgomery's in 2004.

Although Steyr were not all that popular in the UK the ERF ES range did in fact utilise the Steyr all-steel cab. This example, being a concrete mixer with Cummins 180 engine, was discharging its load on a small job in Blurton, Stoke on Trent.

As mentioned earlier in the book, M.S. Wayman of Sutton Bridge, Linconshire named their vehicles after the local river Nene. *Nene Galaxy* is in the traditional fleet livery and looked rather resplendent when photographed in the yard on a visit in 1992.

Looking a little workworn and rusty, this Leyland Bison tipper was photographed in Buxton in its final days of service. The photograph was taken on 23 April 1992. According to the DVLA site its tax was due just four days later.

Lorries in Britain: The 1990s 45

Interesting to see the somewhat lack of load restraints on these pallets of bricks – shrink wrap and gravity seemed to be all that was needed. However, the crane has been roped on presumably to stop the arm swinging around. The DAF 2500 eight-wheeler of Canute had a Romford, Essex phone number so was a good way from home when seen at Poplar Café, Lymm.

Back to Ferrybridge Services again, and a vehicle taking a short break before heading for home in Wigan was this close coupled drawbar outfit of Belmont Transport. By this time more and more foreign vehicles were to be seen on the UK roads, this Scania 92M being a typical example.

And, as if to prove a point, we have another Scania 92M drawbar outfit. This one was caught on the pumps taking on fuel before continuing its journey with a John Deere combine harvester on board. R.O. Manners & Son from Alnwick, Northumberland are the UK's largest breakers of combines and sell new and second-hand parts worldwide.

Pearson's Transport from Aldermans Green, Coventry is well known for having a fine working fleet of tippers, as well as a number of excellent preserved lorries. Big Foden fans, this S83 eight-wheel tipper certainly had plenty of bling on it.

Over in Yaxley, this Volvo F12 of Peterborough Heavy Haulage was sitting in the yard loaded with a large crawler crane. The piece of equipment between the unit and trailer is known as a 'jeep dolly' and is to help spread the weight of hefty load.

A trip to Cornwall in 1993 saw the author making a visit to Cornwall Commercials of Brighton Cross near Truro. The owners very kindly pulled out this Scammell Crusader recovery vehicle to enable another lorry to be recorded on film for posterity.

Approximately 5 miles from St Helens is the village of Rainford where F. & G. Pye were based. This Seddon Atkinson Strato is loaded with two specialised pallets to carry sheets of glass, as can be seen by the tarpaulins the loads originate from Pilkington's, St Helens, one of the largest manufacturers of specialised glass.

Yet another Scania 82M drawbar outfit. This unidentified combination was parked in a yard at Sandford Hill, Longton, Stoke on Trent in what was then the W. & J. Wass (Sandford Hill Haulage) yard. Since then, the property has become the First Bus company's main depot for the area.

Another Swedish drawbar combination, this time with a Volvo FL10 providing the motive power. The vehicle had purposely been left in this position by request to enable the photo to be taken. It was captured on a weekend in Staples yard in Sleaford, back in 1992.

Up North Combine is a racing pigeon organisation with over twenty-three member federations. Based in Hartlepool this is one of the vehicles that they owned, a DAF 2100 with a drawbar trailer. Both the lorry and trailer are fitted out with facilities for the welfare of homing pigeons. It was seen in a lay-by near Ferrybridge on the A1 probably heading home after releasing the pigeons further south.

In the livery of GEC Distribution this Faun Goliath heavy haulage tractor is seen in the Abnormal Load Engineering (A.L.E.) yard at Common Road, Stafford. These powerful machines were on station to provide traction for the many transformers that were built in the nearby GEC factory.

Another Faun heavy haulage outfit, this time in the Abnormal Load Engineering livery. This model was the 'Koloss' and is seen awaiting its next duty in the abnormal load refuge on the A50 just outside Uttoxeter. It is highly likely that the outfit was waiting to travel to the GEC factory at Stafford, approximately 15 miles away.

One of the many ERF EC lorries that were owned by the excavator manufacturers JCB Ltd. This one had just received its paint job before going into service in 1997. Always kept immaculate, the JCB lorries were only retired in 2021 with many being snapped up at the disposal auction that was held in September that year.

In the JCB corporate livery is this MAN 26.414 artic low-loader of Brit-European from Scholar Green. Most JCB movements are done by this company including Continental deliveries. When captured by the camera on Uttoxeter lorry park it had a Fendt tractor on board, which would possibly have been a backload from their factory in Germany.

Loaded with construction equipment this Leyland DAF 95. 400 over from Northern Ireland was taking a breather at the Ferrybridge Service area in June 1992. Presumably it had come over to collect the assortment of kit for resale back home.

Terberg from Utrecht, Netherlands is a specialist types vehicle builder. This eight-wheel drive recovery vehicle features a 'Club of Four' cab that was used by Volvo, Renault, Saviem and Magirus-Deutz. A brute of a machine, one person referred to it as a 'Volvo on steroids', but it would no doubt have been a very handy piece of kit.

A holiday to Cornwall mid-1993 and when doing the tourist thing the author spotted these two vehicles down at the small port of Charlestown near St Austell. The first is an unidentified DAF 3300 coupled to a rental van trailer.

The second, also coupled to a hire trailer, was a Ford Transcontinental. The small port was traditionally for the loading of china clay, however these two were actually unloading props for the film production of *The Three Musketeers*.

Seen more in the UK on ERF lorries was the all-steel Steyr cab. However, a small number of Austrian-built Steyr lorries were in service with a number of UK operators. This 17S21 was in use with a Stoke on Trent engineering company.

Kellogg's are probably the best-known cereal manufacturer in the world. The company has two plants in the UK, one at Wrexham and one at Trafford Park, Manchester. This Volvo FH12 340 close coupled drawbar outfit, with demountable bodies was between duties at the Poplar Café, Lymm not long after the facility had been opened.

Although the address on the door is for Middleton, Manchester this Foden 4350 (fleet number 166) of Harrison & Jones was photographed in the Alfreton, Derby's depot. Of interest are the telescopic bodies that elevated to load foam, which was then compressed when the bodies were lowered.

When you have a large yard, and lorries need to be kept moving, it makes sense to have a gritter on your fleet. This ex-Department of Transport Foden was located at the North Midlands Co-Op site in Talke, Stoke on Trent. The cab was a modified version of the S83 and was designated S85. No doubt a handy asset.

Renishaw Quarry near Sheffield was where a number of Tarmac tippers were to be found. In the 7 T's livery was this Foden 3250 six-wheeler. It was one of several vehicles that were in possession of owner-drivers, this one lettered to H.D. Lind.

In the same location as the previous photograph was this ERF E8 6 x 4 rigid tipper, however this one is sporting the more contemporary livery of the time (1992). Another owner-driver machine, unfortunately the name is too faint to read.

A smart ERF E6 fridge van with rest cab of Wincanton Transport. Named *Garden*, this was kindly positioned for us at the now closed Uttoxeter depot. At one time Uttoxeter had a large Unigate Dairy in the town, most readers will know that Wincanton is the transport section of Unigate.

Another vehicle posed for us by depot staff at Uttoxeter was this ERF E10 artic in the corporate livery for the Happy Shopper chain of retail stores. Like all Wincanton vehicles this one too has a name, this time *Network*. Quite appropriate for the contract.

As a former employee of Shirley's Transport, the author has a particular affection for this well kept fleet of vehicles. Although initially running livestock and general haulage vehicles they now specialise in bulk tankers. This Iveco Eurostar (175 *Beryl*) being a good example.

Shirley's did not purchase many second-hand vehicles, this ex-British Telecom Foden Fleetmaster (96) found its way to the fleet via Harrisons of Bucknall, a small operator that Shirley's took over along with the tipper work. Primarily it ran out of nearby Croxden Gravel.

Lorries in Britain: The 1990s 59

Another of Shirley's on tipping work, the Volvo F10 had been a major player on the fleet and were highly thought of. Fleet number 130 *Zoe* would have been on frontline duties before going into semi-retirement on local tipping work.

This 1972-registered ERF 68GXB (74 *English Rose*) on chassis number 23000 was originally a tanker, later on it was fitted with a flat platform body and later still this curtainside body as seen in the photograph. It has a somewhat cramped sleep pod cab fitted.

Sadly the author did not capture many Bedford TM lorries on camera, namely as they were a little scarce. However, this one of Cooks of Cornwall was photographed for posterity at the Junction 23 truckstop at Shepshed in March 1992.

This Volvo F6 drawbar outfit may have been a little underpowered in this form, however Harker's Removals from Tyne & Wear must have had faith in the old girl as she was seen on duty at Ferrybridge heading south with the driver also undergoing tuition.

Lorries in Britain: The 1990s

Bassett's of Tittensor, Staffordshire had long been users of ERF, Foden and Atkinson motors. It was therefore a natural progression to try Seddon Atkinson after those companies amalgamated in 1970. This 400 series unit (53 *Alison*) is coupled to a specially adapted trailer for the carriage of roof trusses.

At twenty years old this Atkinson Borderer unit (49 *Lulu*) was still in daily use, which shows just how durable these machines were. Bassett's did have an excellent maintenance scheme that no doubt contributed to the long life. This is one of the few on the fleet in corporate livery. BAL stands for Building Adhesives Ltd from nearby Blurton.

Ensor from Sandbach were in the business of concrete block and building material manufacturing. This Leyland Constructor 30-25 was stationed at another depot in Swadlincote, Derbyshire. The Ensor group was a large concern and at one time held a Mercedes Truck dealership in Stoke on Trent.

Delivering on the cobbled backstreets of Sheffield the author had piloted this Mercedes 1617 up from Stoke on Trent with resin-coated foundry sand. The vehicle (93 *Margaret Ann*) was bought second-hand by B. S. Haulage and gave good service. The company closed when the owners retired.

An unidentified Leyland Bison 2 six-wheel tipper that was spotted at Junction 23 truckstop. Considering it was ten years old it seemed to be holding up well, but the Sankey Ergomatic cab was showing signs of rust – something they were prone to.

Another spot at Junction 23, just off the M1, was this Iveco 165-24 close-coupled drawbar outfit. Rega Metal Products are from Biggleswade and manufacture heating and ventilation products. Interesting to note is the hinged front panel on the body to allow the cab to be tilted for maintenance etc.

C.F. Dickinson from Billinghay, Lincolnshire are sadly no longer with us. With a large customer base for goods such as bulk grain and beet pulp, their vehicles were to be seen in many parts of the UK. This Leyland Roadtrain 17-32 (120) with a tri-axle tipping trailer was on a weekend break in the yard back in May 1995.

Stirling Lloyd are involved in the application of surface dressings and waterproofing. For a while they had a depot at Harpur Hill near Buxton, Derbyshire, where this DAF 2700 was spotted one weekend. Note how the Leyland name had been added to the badge since the takeover.

Another useful machine to have when operating fleets of vehicles is, of course, a suitable recovery vehicle. This Foden eight-wheeler was on standby for Barlow & Hodgkinson at their yard in the small Derbyshire hamlet of Biggin by Hartington. The company is no longer in business.

A visit to Tipcon in Harrogate took place in 1992 and while lots of vehicle were on show in the hall, it was not the best place to take photographs. But all was not lost, as this Seddon Atkinson Strato waste compactor was to be seen outside. *The Predator* certainly looked the part. The Dunlop representative had been busy with the tyre stickers!

Here we have a workworn Leyland Bison six-wheel tipper of Mitchell's from the isle of Portland, Dorset. Complete with diesel stains on the fuel tank it is seen here in its natural environment in one of the quarries that exist on the island. A true workhorse.

Very often parked up in Uttoxeter on a Sunday were vehicles that had trunked down from Scotland with loads of foodstuffs. This Seddon Atkinson Strato artic fridge van of East Coast Roadways, Aberdeen was a regular visitor. As the curtains in the cab were closed the driver would no doubt be having a good sleep after the long journey south.

A school playing field may not seem the usual place to see lorries, but this brand new Leyland Constructor 30-25 was taken along to a small vehicle exhibition at Winton School in Andover, Hampshire. It has a 'rolonof' type skip body for the movement of waste products.

Barnes & Tipping Ltd from Clitheroe, Lancashire were more often to be seen coupled to bulk tipping trailers. To catch one on film with a flat, sheeted trailer loaded with what looks to be reels of paper was a little different. The ERF C Series with added sun-visor certainly looked well.

Another lorry still in service at a mere twenty-three years old was this Commer VC of Refractory Boiler Service from Fenton, Stoke on Trent. It was indeed a rare sight in the early 1990s to see such a vehicle still in use. The company has since closed.

This Volvo F7 6 x 2 unit was one of a number built for Shell and used on fuel deliveries. This example passed to Bugle Transport from Roche, Cornwall and had just brought up a multi-drop load of china clay to the Stoke on Trent area. It was caught on camera in nearby Cheadle.

Lorries in Britain: The 1990s 69

Elliott Transport Services (ETS) of Shepshed are part-load specialists and had a number of contracts on distribution work throughout the UK. A visit to the yard in 1992 saw this Seddon Atkinson 301 curtainsider having a well-earned weekend rest.

Also, at rest for the weekend was no fewer than three ERF E10 rigid eight-wheel curtainsiders. An absolute joy for the enthusiast, this is one example. The vehicle to the left is another of the trio and is in Blue Hawk livery, a company that makes items such as plaster products and mortar.

As well as the influx of European vehicles, there was also an attempt by the Japanese concern of Hino to infiltrate the UK market. Although the company was well established, they never really got a foothold. It was a surprise to find a couple local to the author in use with a contracting company – this is the FS six-wheel model.

And the other Hino at Laidrite was this FY eight-wheel tipper. Apparently, the cab roof lights changed colour when at speed. The company also had a White Road Commander. Unfortunately, the company are no longer in business.

W. Keith & Son Ltd from Flookburgh, Grange-over-Sands, Cumbria were a long-established haulage company and at one time had a number of interesting vehicles including some they converted. However, by the time this Leyland Roadtrain was seen at the Poplar Café, Lymm in 1993 they were using standard outfits. The company was dissolved in 2017.

This Foden 4450 of C. & C. Storey was captured in a lay-by on the old A50 just outside Uttoxeter, the road was later upgraded and the lay-by disappeared under the new road scheme. Storey's were from Cromer over in Norfolk, so the driver may have been heading home after a night's sleep.

This Leyland DAF 95 8 x 4 tractor unit of L.C. Lewis from Newport, Gwent was built to special order in Holland and was plated for 150 tonnes. *Prince William* made a visit to a small vehicle event held in Andover, Hampshire when just over a year old.

This fine-looking drawbar outfit of C.E. Cooke of Leighton, near Crewe, was purchased new from the Stoke on Trent dealers Beech's Garage. It was used to collect produce from the wholesale markets and brought back to Crewe for resale to shops and traders.

Lorries in Britain: The 1990s 73

Unfortunately, the operator of this Foden S80 rigid eight-wheel flat platform lorry proved to be elusive and to this day remains a mystery! A rather plain-looking vehicle it was still in service at seventeen years old and was often seen parked at this location at Arclid, near Sandbach, Cheshire.

George Barker Ltd hailed from London and remained in the transport business until 2012. This Seddon Atkinson with a fridge van trailer was on Sandbach Services in 1992. Interesting to see the London phone numbers differ, the trailer being the old code and the unit having the new code for 'Outer London'.

Again, Poplar Café, Lymm and another company that are sadly no longer with us. Bill Chippington Haulage of St Albans, Hertfordshire and Corby, Northamptonshire had a nicely turned-out fleet with this ERF E14 proclaiming to be their *Flagship*. A shame to see some of these companies now missing off the UK road network.

Buy one get one free? Two Foden rigid eight-wheel tippers of Walter Forshaw Ltd on the Poplar Café with the drivers enjoying a chinwag while taking their break. From Westhoughton, Greater Manchester the company have interests in both demolition and haulage, and have over eighty years' experience.

Charles Wright & Sons of Old Leake in Lincolnshire are agricultural merchants and were formed way back in 1923. The company mill and sell animal feeds and are very active during the sugar beet season. This AEC Marshal six-wheel bulk tipper, although not on frontline service, was at the time (1992) still called up for the occasional duty.

This Scammell CR100 Amazon had suffered the indignity of a breakdown on a motorway service area. If I remember correctly, it had a brake problem (maybe an air-pack failure). It was one of two operated by the Ministry of Defence and was based at Shoeburyness, Essex.

Another company no longer with us is Onward Distribution. This Seddon Atkinson Strato, fleet number 417, shows the old school way of a traditional loaded trailer with a main sheet and 'fly' sheet on top. It was seen taking a break in June 1993 at Poplar Café, Lymm.

Ansell's Brewery merged with Taylor Walker and Ind Coope in 1961 to form Allied Breweries. This smart ERF E6 (5056) with curtainside body was photographed at the Bourne, Lincolnshire distribution depot. Ansell's main brewery was in Aston, Birmingham, but it closed in 1981.

At eleven years old this Leyland Lynx 2 of T. A. Smith & Co. (TASCO) from Spalding, Lincolnshire was still giving good service. It has a load of empty produce boxes on board, which would be used to convey their goods from the field to the processing plants and wholesale markets.

With all those beds on board one would wonder why this DAF 2100 drawbar outfit would have a sleeper pod! Relyon is an old established company and was founded in 1858. Its headquarters are at Wellington, Shropshire. The bodies are of the demountable type, which are handy in the distribution trade. Sandbach Services, 11 March 1993.

Walter Carefoot & Sons (Transport) Ltd are still very much alive and kicking today. Very active with bulk tippers this Leyland Constructor 30-30 faced the author's camera on a visit to the yard in Longridge, Preston, back in 1993. Note the small Leyland DAF badge on the door.

And on the same day, also having a weekend rest, was this Leyland DAF 95 4 x 2 unit coupled to a bulk tipping trailer. By now the influence of DAF over Leyland is reflected in the Leyland name being the lesser of the two.

A little unusual was this single-axle triple dropside trailer coupled to a British Aerospace Leyland Cruiser. Presumably this was a special build for the carriage of particular aircraft components. The Cruiser of course being a lighter unit compared to its big brother the Roadtrain.

Seen tipping a load of washed singles from the local Hem Heath colliery was this ex-British Coal ERF C25 six-wheeler of D.H. (Harry) Kinder from Cheadle, Staffordshire. It was at the authors' place of work, also in Cheadle, and the coal was for the bank of underfeed stokers. Sad to say none of these companies continue to trade!

M336 *Eugenie* on the hymn sheet at Eddie Stobart was this smart-looking Leyland DAF 95 with a sleeper pod on the cab roof. The building in the background may give the location away as the Burton on Trent depot. Prominent on the skyline was the SKOL lager tower at the nearby brewery, which is now owned by Coors, an American company founded in 1873.

Very much an interloper at the time at Sam Longson's, Chapel-en-le-Frith was this DAF 2800 4 x 2 tractor unit. As far as is known it was the only example of a DAF on the fleet until later years, when the CF came on board. The fleet was almost 100 per cent ERF in those days; the DAF is coupled to a trailer in Ferodo livery, a nearby customer.

A rare example of a Dennison tractor unit, which was seen at a vintage rally carrying tractors. Dennison are still in business to this day as trailer manufacturers. These tractor units were built in Ireland and the cab was from the Finnish manufacturer Sisu. Early Dennisons were fitted with a motor panels cab and the majority had Rolls-Royce engines.

Another bit of an oddball motor was this Leyland Lynx 2 of Fegg Hayes Pottery Ltd. It has a sleeper pod over the cab. These pods were accessory units made by Hatcher who also supplied goods such as air horns. The family-run pottery wholesale company still exists, but no longer runs their own transport.

Hills of Pyebridge in Derbyshire had this Leyland DAF 95-400 200 tonne tractor unit on their fleet. It was the third such vehicle to enter service with them and on this occasion and was seen in 1991 taking a breather on a service area on the M1. Quite an appropriate number plate for the impressive outfit.

The large dairy complex at Fole, near Uttoxeter has long since closed and was demolished in 2018. The large fleet of vehicles stationed there included milk collection tankers and vehicles like this Foden S104 (S10 Mk 3 cab) that was part of the retail and inter-depot delivery division. It is coupled to a refrigerated curtainside trailer, which were referred to as 'Insuliners'.

On a night out at Checkley rest and station, in Staffordshire, this Volvo F6 is a special build vehicle and was used as seen with a drawbar trailer by Calor (11230) to deliver and install gas tanks. These were obviously not heavy, hence the use of the out of proportion trailer and only a 6-litre engine.

Markham Moor Services, near Retford on the A1, was the stopping place for this Volvo FL6 drawbar outfit of Tufcon Containers from Scarborough. The 6-litre engine would have enough grunt to cope with the lightweight load.

A much-missed fleet on the UK roads is that of Brian Harris from Devon. *Widecombe Warrior* was just pulling off the fuel pump at the old Poplar Café, Lymm. Always well turned out this fine E Series ERF epitomises the fleet at that time, unfortunately the environmentalists won the day and contributed to the closure of the company in 2001.

Chas. Armstrong & Son from London ran a very tidy fleet including this Leyland Lynx which had stopped in Tunstall, Stoke on Trent for the driver to seek directions. On contract to Alpha Lighting (also London) it was certainly in good order for a vehicle that was twelve years old.

Philip Maddison is one of life's characters and on this visit to the yard in Coningsby, Lincolnshire back in 1992 he very kindly took time out to have a chat about lorries, and here he is on board a nice Foden 4300 eight-wheel tipper that he positioned in a suitable pose for a photograph. A true gent.

A tour around the Dorset area in 1993 and this Scammell Routeman Mk 3 tipper was spotted in Poole. Looking a little workworn, it was in fact still taxed for the road. It exemplifies a typical vehicle from the era with all the dirt and grime – an enthusiast's delight!

Although lettered to an address in Alresford, Hampshire this Leyland Lynx 2 of Hampshire Watercress was in fact seen at the company premises in Andover. The company supplies watercress throughout the UK, Vitacress being the company brand name. The area is well known for the product and the preserved railway in the county is actually known as the Watercress Line.

Walter Day & Sons from Thurlby in Lincolnshire have traded as livestock hauliers for over eighty years. Calling at the yard it was nice to catch this DAF 2700 six-wheeler. Unfortunately on the day it wasn't coupled up to the drawbar trailer that it often pulled. Still a good-looking motor.

Lorries in Britain: The 1990s 87

The author likes to see proper drawbar outfits like this Volvo F6 of Alstons Furniture. The outfit was delivering furniture in Cheadle, Staffordshire. It may have been a 'just in time' delivery as some items were transferred straight onto the van that can be seen in the background.

And another Volvo drawbar outfit, this time an FL6 of Walkers, the famous crisp makers from Leicester. Founded in 1948, the company holds over 50 per cent of the British crisp market and this outfit would be more than able to cope with the light bulky load of snack foods. Seen at Sandbach Services, M6, 1993.

Fleet number 3287, an ERF E Series of Sutton & Son of St Helens is seen having a breather at Sandbach. A well-known company, it was established back in 1926 by Alf Sutton. Over the years it has developed into a major player with several acquisitions and has a number of operations abroad including Asia, USA and the Middle East.

Sam Satterthwaite of Streetly Garage was a long established Foden dealer. On the occasion of his ninetieth birthday a gathering of Foden vehicles was arranged to celebrate this milestone. This artic of Harpers came along with a Foden steam tractor on board, which added to the atmosphere of the day.

Sam Ostle from Kirkby Stephen, Cumbria had a nice fleet of vehicles, and a livery that stood out with its fluorescent lettering. Unfortunately, the livery was lost when the company was taken over by Turners of Soham. *Eden Prince*, a Leyland DAF 95 with a powder tank trailer, was captured for posterity at Markham Moor Services on 16 June 1992.

Another Sam Ostle Leyland DAF 95 was this outfit seen on the old Poplar Café at Lymm. It is in the customer livery of Cape boards, which is a product for use in the building industry. This vehicle, *Eden Mark*, is another that incorporates the name of the River Eden that flows through Cumbria.

W.J. Riding had a traditional and very distinctive livery – again, this was to destined to disappear from our roads. Most if not all the vehicles were given a name and fleet number, in this instance Seddon Atkinson 401 was *Mammoth* (40), which was coupled up to trailer number 181 and on contract to ICI Petrochemicals.

Another vehicle of Riding's and from the Seddon Atkinson stable was this 4-11 unit coupled to a tautliner trailer. Number 18 *Apollo* has been adorned with a couple of Knights Head badges on the front panel. These used to be fitted to the Atkinson range prior to the merger with Seddon that took place in the early 1970s.

The immaculate fleet of Gibbs of Fraserburgh is yet another company no longer with us – they closed in 2002 due to a downturn in business. This fine Leyland DAF 95 *Flower of Scotland*, was at the Poplar Café at Lymm before continuing its journey south in 1993.

A C Series ERF of Hayes Roadways Ltd, from Brierley Hill, was captured on film in March 1993 on the Sandbach Service area while taking a break. It has a sleeper cab and a 'tag' axle. It's quite possible that this was a converted tractor unit.

Allied Distribution Services Ltd owned this Seddon Atkinson Strato (96243), taking a breather at Markham Moor before continuing with its load. The trailer is lettered to a product made by Goldwell's in Kent. 'Pink Lady' is actually a pear cider and not made from Pink Lady apples!

Seen having just parked at The Hollies on Watling Street (A5) at Cannock is this Volvo F12 artic low-loader of Wrekin Transport from Telford. The CAT 775D dump truck weighing approximately 43 tonnes would have been collected from just down the road at Finning's the Caterpillar dealers.

Naylors Transport of Leyland, Lancashire are a well-established company still in business today. This Leyland Roadtrain piloted by *Dave* faced the author's camera while taking a break at the Tamworth Services, which is situated on the M42 and close to the A5 (Watling Street). Of note is the DAF name appearing on the cab door badge.

The origins of this vehicle are little known. Certainly the cab is off an A Series tractor unit on chassis number 29033, however the single towing jaw points to an earlier chassis. It was not uncommon for these conversions to be carried out. This belonged to Barlow's, scrap metal merchants in Uttoxeter, Staffordshire, who ran it quite late.

At one time F. Swain & Sons Ltd had quite a sizeable fleet. Based at Adlington, between Macclesfield and Hazel Grove, they were involved in not only transport but also storage and warehouse facilities. This MAN six-wheel curtainsider was in the yard when the company was visited in 1999. The company was dissolved in 2020.

Quite a rare beast, this Ford Cargo 'Chinese six' curtainside was operated by Nelsons of Durham. This photograph was taken on Sandbach Services in 1991. The sleeper pod atop the cab must have been a bit cramped, but no doubt served its purpose. The Iveco badge highlights the fact that they formed a merger with Ford (1986), the Cargo being updated and renamed the Eurocargo in 1991.

Acknowledgements

Although all of these photographs were taken by the author, it was often in the company of fellow enthusiasts.

Not only were they good company, but also a mine of information on certain aspects like the location of yards, company and vehicle details, etc.

To this end I thank the following: George Barker, Ian Moxon, Malcolm Mortimer, Neil Matlock, John Andrew, John Heath, Geoff Hinchliffe, and Michael Marshall. We certainly covered some miles.

Also, I must thank members of the Historic Commercial Vehicle Society, the now disbanded Fifth Wheel Lorry Club, The Commercial Vehicle and Road Transport Club, The ERF Society, The Foden Society, The Scammell Register and all the enthusiasts I have had the pleasure to meet along the way.

I will be forever grateful.